Make It Happen

Make It Happen

The Blueprint for Initiative, Leadership, & Success

ELBERT HUBBARD & PETER KYNE

A Message to Garcia, published in 1899 by Elbert Hubbard.

The Go-Getter, published in 1922 by Peter B. Kyne.

Reprint edition by Sound Wisdom, 2025

Cover design and interior page design, copyright 2025. All rights reserved.

This book is a historical artifact. Sound Wisdom has reprinted this work to preserve and share the best wisdom handed down from great men and women in history. Not all of the ideas and beliefs held by these authors remain acceptable in our present time, and Sound Wisdom does not condone or endorse every belief shared within this book. We encourage readers to glean the best timeless wisdom from these pages, while exercising grace toward our ancestors' flaws and forgiveness toward the mistakes of the past.

ISBN 13 TP: 978-1-64095-690-2

ISBN 13 eBook: 978-1-64095-691-9

1 2025

Contents

Introduction to Make It Happen 7

A Message to Garcia by Elbert Hubbard 9

   A Message to Garcia 11

Life Lessons by Elbert Hubbard 19

   A Prayer 21

   Lesson 1: Time and Chance 23

   Lesson 2: One-Man Power 27

   Lesson 3: Mental Attitude 31

   Lesson 4: The Folly of Living in the Future 35

   Lesson 5: The Spirit of Man 37

   Lesson 6: Initiative 41

   Lesson 7: The Neutral 43

   Lesson 8: Sympathy, Knowledge, and Poise 45

   Lesson 9: Love and Faith 49

   Lesson 10: Giving Something for Nothing 51

   Lesson 11: Work and Waste 55

Lesson 12: The Law of Obedience................57

From Garcia to The Go-Getter 59

**The Go-Getter: A Story That Tells You
How to Be One** by Peter B. Kyne 61

Peter B. Kyne's Dedication........................63

Chapter I 65

Chapter II......................................73

Chapter III.....................................85

Chapter IV.....................................89

Chapter V......................................93

Conclusion: The Blueprint of the Doer 117
About Elbert Hubbard 119
About Peter B. Kyne 121

Introduction to Make It Happen

In a world full of talkers, *Make It Happen* celebrates the doers.

What sets apart those who succeed from those who stall, hesitate, or make excuses? It's initiative. It's follow-through. It's that inner fire that drives a person to figure it out, get it done, and take full responsibility without waiting for instructions or praise. This book brings together two of the most enduring and powerful fables on action and accountability: *A Message to Garcia* and *The Go-Getter*.

First published in 1899, *A Message to Garcia* by Elbert Hubbard shares the example of a man who was given an impossible mission—deliver a message deep into enemy territory, without clear directions—and succeeded, without question, hesitation, or delay. Rowan, the soldier in the story, became a symbol for initiative and reliability.

As Hubbard put it, "McKinley gave Rowan a letter to be delivered to Garcia; Rowan took the letter and did not ask, 'Where is he at?'" That level of action, purpose, and resolve is still rare—and still needed.

Peter B. Kyne's *The Go-Getter*, first published in 1922, picks up where Hubbard leaves off. It's a humorous but meaningful story of a disabled World War I veteran named Bill Peck who refuses to accept failure. Faced with a rigged test meant to frustrate and discourage him, Peck battles all obstacles—misdirection, bureaucracy, and even physical pain—to deliver a blue vase. Why? Because he said he would. He's a go-getter. And, like Rowan, he represents the mindset and spirit of someone who doesn't wait around for conditions to be perfect.

These two stories have inspired generations of leaders, soldiers, entrepreneurs, and change-makers. Their message is timeless: excuses don't build anything—but initiative, ownership, and grit do.

Before you read these short classics, ask yourself: Am I a person who can be trusted with the mission? Will I find a way, or find an excuse?

A Message to Garcia

ELBERT HUBBARD

A Message to Garcia

In all this Cuban business, there is one man stands out on the horizon of my memory like Mars at perihelion.

When war broke out between Spain and the United States, it was very necessary to communicate quickly with the leader of the Insurgents. Garcia was somewhere in the mountain fastnesses of Cuba—no one knew where. No mail or telegraph could reach him. The President must secure his cooperation, and quickly. What to do!

Someone said to the President, "There's a fellow by the name of Rowan will find Garcia for you, if anybody can."

Rowan was sent for and given a letter to be delivered to Garcia. How "the fellow by the name of Rowan" took the letter, sealed it up in an oil-skin pouch, strapped it over his heart, in four days landed by night off the coast of Cuba from an open boat, disappeared into the jungle, and in three weeks came out on the other side of the island, having traversed a hostile country on foot, and having delivered his letter to Garcia, are things I have no special desire now to tell in detail. The point I wish to make is this: McKinley gave Rowan a letter to be delivered to Garcia; Rowan took the letter and did not ask, "Where is he at?"

By the Eternal! There is a man whose form should be cast in deathless bronze and the statue placed in every college in the land. It is not book-learning young men need, nor instruction about this or that, but a stiffening of the vertebrae which will cause them to be loyal to a trust, to act promptly, concentrate their energies, do the thing: "Carry a message to Garcia!"

General Garcia is dead now, but there are other Garcias. No man who has endeavored to carry out an enterprise where many hands were needed, but has been well-nigh appalled at times by the imbecility of the average man—the inability or unwillingness to concentrate on a thing and do it.

Slipshod assistance, foolish inattention, dowdy indifference, and half-hearted work seemed the rule; and no man succeeds unless by hook or crook, or threat, he forces or bribes other men to assist him; or mayhap, God and His goodness performs a miracle, and sends him an Angel of Light for an assistant. You, reader, put this matter to a test: You are sitting now in your office—six clerks are within your call. Summon any one and make this request, "Please look in the encyclopedia and make a brief memorandum for me concerning the life of Correggio."

Will the clerk quietly say, "Yes, sir," and go do the task?

On your life, he will not. He will look at you out of a fishy eye, and ask one or more of the following questions:

- Who was he?
- Which encyclopedia?
- Where is the encyclopedia?
- Was I hired for that?
- Don't you mean Bismarck?
- What's the matter with Charlie doing it?
- Is he dead?
- Is there any hurry?
- Shan't I bring you the book and let you look it up yourself?
- What do you want to know for?

And I will lay you ten to one that after you have answered the questions, and explained how to find the information, and why you want it, the clerk will go off and get one of the other clerks to help him find Garcia—and then come back and tell you there is no such man. Of course, I may lose my bet, but according to the Law of Average, I will not.

Now, if you are wise, you will not bother to explain to your assistant that Correggio is indexed under the Cs, not in the Ks, but you will smile sweetly and say, "Never mind," and go look it up yourself. And this incapacity for independent action, this moral stupidity, this infirmity of the will, this unwillingness to cheerfully catch hold and lift, are the things that put pure socialism so far into the future. If men will not act for themselves, what will they do if the benefit of their effort is for all.

A first mate with knotted club seems necessary; and the dread of getting "the bounce" Saturday night holds many a worker in his place.

Advertise for a stenographer, and nine times out of ten who apply can neither spell nor punctuate–and do not think it necessary to.

Can such a one write a letter to Garcia?

"You see that bookkeeper," said the foreman to me in a large factory.

"Yes, what about him?"

"Well, he's a fine accountant, but if I'd send him to town on an errand, he might accomplish the errand all right, and, on the other hand, might stop at four saloons on the way, and when he got to Main Street, would forget what he had been sent for."

Can such a man be entrusted to carry a message to Garcia?

We have recently been hearing much maudlin sympathy expressed for the "down-trodden denizen of the sweat shop" and the "homeless wanderer searching for honest employment," and with it all often go many hard words for the men in power.

Nothing is said about the employer who grows old before his time in a vain attempt to get frowsy ne'er-do-wells to do intelligent work; and his long patient striving with "help" that does nothing but loaf when his back is turned. In every store and factory, there is a constant weeding-out process going on. The employer is constantly sending away "help" that have shown their incapacity to further the interests of the business, and others are being taken on.

No matter how good times are, this sorting continues, only if times are hard and work is scarce, this sorting is done finer—but out and forever out, the incompetent and unworthy go. It is the survival of the fittest. Self-interest prompts every employer to keep the best—those who can carry a message to Garcia.

I know one man of really brilliant parts who has not the ability to manage a business of his own, and yet who is absolutely worthless to anyone else, because he carries with him constantly the insane suspicion that his employer is oppressing or intending to oppress him. He cannot give orders and he will not receive them. Should a message be given him to take to Garcia, his answer would probably be, "Take it yourself."

Tonight this man walks the street looking for work. The wind whistling through his threadbare coat. No one who knows him dare employ him, for he is a regular firebrand of discontent. He is impervious to reason, and the only thing that can impress him is the toe of a thick soled Number Nine boot.

Of course, I know that one so morally deformed is no less to be pitied than a physical cripple; but in your pitying, let us drop a tear, too, for the men who are striving to carry on a great enterprise, whose working hours are not limited by the whistle, and whose hair is fast turning white through the struggle to hold the line in dowdy indifference, slipshod imbecility, and the heartless in gratitude which, but for their enterprise, would be both hungry and homeless.

Have I put the matter too strongly? Possibly I have; but when all the world has gone a-slumming I wish to speak a word of sympathy for the man who succeeds—the man who, against great odds, has directed the efforts of others, and, having succeeded, finds there's nothing in it: nothing but bare board and clothes. I have carried a dinner-pale and worked for a day's wages, and I have also been an employer of labor, and I know there is something to be said on both sides. There is no excellence, per se, in poverty; rags are no recommendation; and all employers are not rapacious and high-handed, any more than all poor men are virtuous.

My heart goes out to the man who does his work, when the "boss" is away, as well as when he is home. And the man who, when given a letter for Garcia, quietly takes the missive, without asking any idiotic questions, and with no lurking intention of chucking it into the nearest sewer or of doing aught else but deliver it, never gets "laid off," nor has to go on strike for higher wages. Civilization is one long anxious search for just such individuals. Anything such a man asks will be granted. His kind is so rare that no employer can afford to let him go. He is wanted in every city, town, and village—in every office, shop, store, and factory. The world cries out for such; he is needed, and needed badly—the man who can carry *a message to Garcia.*

Life Lessons

ELBERT HUBBARD

A Prayer

The supreme prayer of my heart is not to be learned, rich, famous, powerful, or "good," but simply to be radiant. I desire to radiate health, cheerfulness, calm courage, and good will. I wish to live without hate, whim, jealousy, envy, fear. I wish to be simple, honest, frank, natural, clean in mind and clean in body, unaffected—ready to say, "I do not know," if it be so, and to meet all men on an absolute equality—to face any obstacle and meet every difficulty unabashed and unafraid.

I wish others to live their lives, too—up to their highest, fullest, and best. To that end I pray that I may never meddle, interfere, dictate, give advice that is not wanted, or assist when my services are not needed. If I can help people, I'll do it by giving them a chance to help themselves; and if I can uplift or inspire, let it be by example, inference, and suggestion, rather than by injunction and dictation. That is to say, I desire to be radiant—to radiate life.

Lesson 1

Time and Chance

As the subject is somewhat complex, I will have to explain it to you. The first point is that there is not so very much difference in the intelligence of people after all. The great person is not so great as folks think, and the dull person is not quite so stupid as they seem. The difference in our estimates of people lies in the fact that one individual is able to get their goods into the show-window, and the other is not aware that they have any show-window or any goods.

"The soul knows all things, and knowledge is only a remembering," says Emerson.

This seems a very broad statement; and yet the fact remains that the vast majority of people know a thousand times as much as they are aware of. Far down in the silent depths of subconsciousness lie myriads of truths, each awaiting a time when its owner shall call it forth. To utilize these stored-up thoughts, you must express them to others; and to be able to express them well your soul has to soar into this subconscious realm where you have cached these net results of experience.

In other words, you must "come out"—get out of self—away from self-consciousness, into the region of partial oblivion—away from the boundaries of time and the limitations of space. The great painter forgets all in the presence of his canvas; the writer is oblivious to his surroundings; the singer floats away on the wings of melody (and carries the audience with her); the orator pours out his soul for an hour, and it seems to him as if barely five minutes had passed, so rapt is he in his exalted theme. When you reach the heights of sublimity and are expressing your highest and best, you are in a partial trance condition. And all those who enter this condition surprise themselves by the quantity of knowledge and the extent of insight they possess. And some going a little deeper than others into this trance condition, and having no knowledge of the miraculous storing up of truth in the subconscious cells, jump to the conclusion that their intelligence is guided by a spirit not theirs. When one reaches this conclusion they begin to wither at the top, for they rely on the dead, and cease to feed the well-springs of their subconscious self.

The mind is a dual affair—objective and subjective. The objective mind sees all, hears all, reasons things out. The subjective mind stores up and only gives out when the objective mind sleeps. And as few people ever cultivate the absorbed, reflective, or semi-trance state, where the objective mind rests, they never really call on their subconscious treasury for its stores. They are always self-conscious.

A man in commerce, where men prey on their kind, must be alive and alert to what is going on, or while he dreams, his competitor will seize upon his birthright. And so you see why poets are poor and artists often beg.

And the summing up of this sermonette is that all people are equally rich, only some through fate are able to muster their mental legions on the plains of their being and count them, while others are never able to do so.

But what think you is necessary before a person can come into full possession of their subconscious treasures? Well, I'll tell you: It is not ease, nor prosperity, nor requited love, nor worldly security—not these.

"You sing well," said the master, impatiently, to his best pupil, "but you will never sing divinely until you have given your all for love, and then been neglected and rejected, and scorned and beaten, and left for dead. Then, if you do not exactly die, you will come back, and when the world hears your voice it will mistake you for an angel and fall at your feet."

And the moral is, that as long as you are satisfied and comfortable, you use only the objective mind and live in the world of sense. But let love be torn from your grasp and flee as a shadow, living only as a memory in a haunting sense of loss; let death come and the sky shut down over less worth in the world; or stupid misunderstanding and crushing defeat grind you into the dust—then you may arise, forgetting time and space and self, and take refuge in mansions not made with hands; and find a certain sad, sweet satisfaction in the contemplation of treasures stored up where moth and rust do not corrupt, and where thieves do not break through and steal.

And thus looking out into the Eternal, you entirely forget the present and go forth into the Land of Subconsciousness—the Land of Spirit, where yet dwell the gods of ancient and innocent days. Is it worth the cost?

Lesson 2

One-Man Power

Every successful concern is the result of a One-Man Power. Cooperation, technically, is an iridescent dream—things cooperate because the individual makes them. He cements them by his will.

But find this Man, and get his confidence, and his weary eyes will look into yours and the cry of his heart shall echo in your ears. "O, for someone to help me bear this burden!"

Then he will tell you of his endless search for Ability, and of his continual disappointments and thwartings in trying to get someone to help himself by helping him.

Ability is the one crying need of the hour. The banks are bulging with money, and everywhere are people looking for work. The harvest is ripe. But the Ability to captain the unemployed and utilize the capital is lacking—sadly lacking. In every city there are many five- and ten-thousand-dollar-a-year positions to be filled, but the only applicants are men who want jobs at fifteen dollars a week. Your man of Ability has a place already. Yes, Ability is a rare article.

But there is something that is much scarcer, something finer far, something rarer than this quality of Ability.

It is the ability to recognize Ability.

The sternest comment that ever can be made against employers as a class lies in the fact that people of Ability usually succeed in showing their worth in spite of their employer, and not with his assistance and encouragement.

If you know the lives of people of Ability, you know that they discovered their power, almost without exception, through chance or accident. Had the accident not occurred that made the opportunity, the person would have remained unknown and practically lost to the world. The experience of Tom Potter, telegraph operator at an obscure little way station, is truth painted large. That fearful night, when most of the wires were down and a passenger train went through the bridge, gave Tom Potter the opportunity of discovering himself. He took charge of the dead, cared for the wounded, settled fifty claims—drawing drafts on the company—burned the last vestige of the wreck, sunk the waste iron in the river and repaired the bridge before the arrival of the Superintendent on the spot.

"Who gave you the authority to do all this?" demanded the Superintendent.

"Nobody," replied Tom, "I assumed the authority."

The next month Tom Potter's salary was five thousand dollars a year, and in three years he was making ten times this, simply because he could get other men to do things.

Why wait for an accident to discover Tom Potter? Let us set traps for Tom Potter, and lie in wait for him. Perhaps Tom Potter is just around the corner, across the street, in the next room, or at our elbow. Myriads of embryonic Tom Potters await discovery and development if we but look for them.

I know a man who roamed the woods and fields for thirty years and never found an Indian arrow. One day he began to think "arrow," and stepping out of his doorway he picked one up. Since then he has collected a bushel of them.

Suppose we cease wailing about incompetence, sleepy indifference and slipshod "help" that watches the clock. These things exist—let us dispose of the subject by admitting it, and then emphasize the fact that freckled farmer boys come out of the West and East and often go to the front and do things in a masterly way. There is one name that stands out in history like a beacon light after all these twenty-five hundred years have passed, just because the man had the sublime genius of discovering Ability. That man is Pericles. Pericles made Athens.

And today the very dust of the streets of Athens is being sifted and searched for relics and remnants of the things made by people who were captained by men of Ability who were discovered by Pericles.

There is very little competition in this line of discovering Ability. We sit down and wail because Ability does not come our way. Let us think "Ability," and possibly we can jostle Pericles there on his pedestal, where he has stood for over a score of centuries—the man with a supreme genius for recognizing Ability. Hail to thee, Pericles, and hail to thee, Great Unknown, who shall be the first to successfully imitate this captain of men.

Lesson 3

Mental Attitude

Success is in the blood. There are those whom fate can never keep down–they march forward in a jaunty manner, and take by divine right the best of everything that the earth affords. But their success is not attained by means of the Samuel Smiles-Connecticut policy. They do not lie in wait, nor scheme, nor fawn, nor seek to adapt their sails to catch the breeze of popular favor. Still, they are ever alert and alive to any good that may come their way, and when it comes they simply appropriate it, and tarrying not, move steadily on.

Good health! Whenever you go out of doors, draw the chin in, carry the crown of the head high, and fill the lungs to the utmost; drink in the sunshine; greet your friends with a smile, and put soul into every hand-clasp.

Do not fear being misunderstood; and never waste a moment thinking about your enemies. Try to fix firmly in your own mind what you would like to do, and then without violence of direction you will move straight to the goal.

Fear is the rock on which we split, and hate the shoal on which many a ship is stranded. When we become fearful, the judgment is as unreliable as the compass of a ship whose hold is full of iron ore; when we hate, we have unshipped the rudder; and if ever we stop to meditate on what the gossips say, we have allowed a hawser to foul the screw.

Keep your mind on the great and splendid thing you would like to do; and then, as the days go gliding by, you will find yourself unconsciously seizing the opportunities that are required for the fulfillment of your desire, just as the coral insect takes from the running tide the elements that it needs. Picture in your mind the able, earnest, useful person you desire to be, and the thought that you hold is hourly transforming you into that particular individual you so admire.

Thought is supreme, and to think is often better than to do.

Preserve a right mental attitude—the attitude of courage, frankness, and good cheer.

Darwin and Spencer have told us that this is the method of Creation. Each animal has evolved the parts it needed and desired. The horse is fleet because he wishes to be; the bird flies because it desires to; the duck has a web foot because it wants to swim. All things come through desire and every sincere prayer is answered. We become like that on which our hearts are fixed.

Many people know this, but they do not know it thoroughly enough so that it shapes their lives. We want friends, so we scheme and chase across lots after strong people, and lie in wait for good folks—or alleged good folks—hoping to be able to attach ourselves to them. The only way to secure friends is to be one. And before you are fit for friendship you must be able to do without it. That is to say, you must have sufficient self-reliance to take care of yourself, and then out of the surplus of your energy you can do for others.

The individual who craves friendship, and yet desires a self-centered spirit more, will never lack for friends.

If you would have friends, cultivate solitude instead of society. Drink in the ozone; bathe in the sunshine; and out in the silent night, under the stars, say to yourself again and yet again, "I am a part of all my eyes behold!" And the feeling then will come to you that you are no mere interloper between earth and heaven; but you are a necessary part of the whole. No harm can come to you that does not come to all, and if you shall go down it can only be amid a wreck of worlds.

Like old Job, that which we fear will surely come upon us. By a wrong mental attitude we have set in motion a train of events that ends in disaster. People who die in middle life from disease, almost without exception, are those who have been preparing for death. The acute tragic condition is simply the result of a chronic state of mind—a culmination of a series of events.

Character is the result of two things—mental attitude, and the way we spend our time. It is what we think and what we do that make us what we are.

By laying hold on the forces of the universe, you are strong with them. And when you realize this, all else is easy, for in your arteries will course red corpuscles, and in your heart the determined resolution is born to do and to be. Carry your chin in and the crown of your head high. We are gods in the chrysalis.

Lesson 4

The Folly of Living in the Future

The question is often asked, "What becomes of all the Valedictorians and all the Class-Day Poets?"

I can give information as to two parties for whom this inquiry is made—the Valedictorian of my class is now a most industrious and worthy floor-walker in Siegel, Cooper & Company's store, and I was the Class-Day Poet. Both of us had our eyes fixed on the Goal. We stood on the Threshold and looked out upon the world preparatory to going forth, seizing it by the tail and snapping its head off for our own delectation.

We had our eyes fixed on the Goal—it might better have been the jail.

It was a very absurd thing for us to fix our eyes on the Goal. It strained our vision and took our attention from our work. We lost our grip on the present.

To think of the Goal is to travel the distance over and over in your mind and dwell on how awfully far off it is. We have so little mind-doing business on such a limited capital of intellect—that to wear it threadbare looking for a far-off thing is to get hopelessly stranded in Siegel, Cooper & Company.

Of course, Siegel, Cooper & Company is all right, too, but the point is this—it wasn't the Goal!

A goodly dash of indifference is a requisite in the formula for doing a great work.

No one knows what the Goal is—we are all sailing under sealed orders.

Do your work today, doing it the best you can, and live one day at a time. The person who does this is conserving their God-given energy, and not spinning it out into tenuous spider threads so fragile and filmy that unkind Fate will probably brush it away.

To do your work well today is the certain preparation for something better tomorrow. The past has gone from us forever; the future we cannot reach; the present alone is ours. Each day's work is a preparation for the next day's duties.

Live in the present—the Day is here, the time is Now.

There is only one thing that is worth praying for—that we may be in the line of Evolution.

Lesson 5

The Spirit of Man

Maybe I am all wrong about it, yet I cannot help believing that the spirit of man will live again in a better world than ours. Fenelon says: "Justice demands another life to make good the inequalities of this." Astronomers prophesy the existence of stars long before they can see them. They know where they ought to be, and training their telescopes in that direction they wait, knowing they shall find them.

Materially, no one can imagine anything more beautiful than this earth, for the simple reason that we cannot imagine anything we have not seen; we may make new combinations, but the whole is made up of parts of things with which we are familiar. This great green earth out of which we have sprung, of which we are a part, that supports our bodies which must return to it to repay the loan, is very, very beautiful.

But the spirit of man is not fully at home here; as we grow in soul and intellect, we hear, and hear again, a voice which says: "Arise and get thee hence, for this is not thy rest." And the greater and nobler and more sublime the spirit, the more constant is the discontent. Discontent may come from various causes, so it will not do to assume that the discontented ones are always the pure in heart, but it is a fact that the wise and excellent have all known the meaning of world-weariness.

The more you study and appreciate this life, the more sure you are that this is not all. You pillow your head upon Mother Earth, listen to her heart-throb, and even as your spirit is filled with the love of her, your gladness is half pain and there comes to you a joy that hurts. To look upon the most exalted forms of beauty, such as sunset at sea, the coming of a storm on the prairie, or the sublime majesty of the mountains, begets a sense of sadness, an increasing loneliness. It is not enough to say that people encroach on others so that we are really deprived of our freedom, that civilization is caused by a bacillus, and that from a natural condition we have gotten into a hurly-burly where rivalry is rife—all this may be true, but beyond and outside of all this there is no physical environment in way of plenty which earth can supply, that will give the tired soul peace. They are the happiest who have the least; and the fable of the stricken king and the shirtless beggar contains the germ of truth. The wise hold all earthly ties very lightly—they are stripping for eternity.

World-weariness is only a desire for a better spiritual condition. There is more to be written on this subject of world-pain—to exhaust the theme would require a book. And certain it is that I have no wish to say the final word on any topic. The gentle reader has certain rights, and among these is the privilege of summing up the case.

But the fact holds that world-pain is a form of desire. All desires are just, proper, and right; and their gratification is the means by which nature supplies us that which we need.

Desire not only causes us to seek that which we need, but is a form of attraction by which the good is brought to us, just as the amoebae create a swirl in the waters that brings their food within reach.

Every desire in nature has a fixed and definite purpose in the Divine Economy, and every desire has its proper gratification. If we desire the close friendship of a certain person, it is because that person has certain soul-qualities that we do not possess, and which complement our own.

Through desire do we come into possession of our own; by submitting to its beckonings we add cubits to our stature; and we also give out to others our own attributes, without becoming poorer, for soul is not limited. All nature is a symbol of spirit, and so I am forced to believe that somewhere there must be a proper gratification for this mysterious nostalgia of the soul.

The Valhalla of the Norseman, the Nirvana of the Hindu, the Heaven of the Christian are natural hopes of beings whose cares and disappointments here are softened by belief that somewhere, Thor, Brahma, or God gives compensation.

The Eternal Unities require a condition where men and women shall be permitted to love and not to sorrow; where the tyranny of things hated shall not prevail, nor that for which the heart yearns turn to ashes at our touch.

Lesson 6

Initiative

The world bestows its big prizes, both in money and honors, for but one thing. And that is Initiative. What is Initiative? I'll tell you: It is doing the right thing without being told. But next to doing the right thing without being told is to do it when you are told once. That is to say, carry the message to Garcia! There are those who never do a thing until they are told twice: such get no honors and small pay. Next, there are those who do the right thing only when necessity kicks them from behind, and these get indifference instead of honors, and a pittance for pay.

This kind spends most of its time polishing a bench with a hard-luck story. Then, still lower down in the scale than this, we find the fellow who will not do the right thing even when someone goes along to show him how, and stays to see that he does it; he is always out of a job, and receives the contempt he deserves, unless he has a rich Pa, in which case

MAKE IT HAPPEN

Destiny awaits nearby with a stuffed club. To which class do you belong?

Lesson 7

The Neutral

There is known to me a prominent business house that by the very force of its directness and worth has incurred the enmity of many rivals. In fact, there is a very general conspiracy on hand to put the institution down and out. In talking with a young man employed by this house, he yawned and said, "Oh, in this quarrel I am neutral."

"But you get your bread and butter from this firm, and in a matter where the very life of the institution is concerned, I do not see how you can be a neutral."

And he changed the subject.

I think that if I enlisted in the Japanese army I would not be a neutral.

Business is a fight—a continual struggle—just as life is. Man has reached his present degree of development through struggle. Struggle there must be and always will be. The struggle began as purely physical; as man evolved it shifted ground to the mental, psychic, and the spiritual, with a few dashes of cave-man proclivities still left. But depend upon it, the struggle will always be—life is activity. And when it gets to be a struggle in well-doing, it will still be a struggle. When inertia gets the better of you it is time to telephone to the undertaker.

The only real neutral in this game of life is a dead one.

Eternal vigilance is not only the price of liberty, but of every other good thing.

A business that is not safeguarded on every side by active, alert, attentive, vigilant people is gone. As oxygen is the disintegrating principle of life, working night and day to dissolve, separate, pull apart, and dissipate, so there is something in business that continually tends to scatter, destroy, and shift possession from this one to that. A million mice nibble eternally at every business venture.

The mice are not neutrals, and if enough employees in a business house are neutrals, the whole concern will eventually come tumbling about their ears.

I like that order of Field-Marshal Oyama: "Give every honorable neutral that you find in our lines the honorable boot."

Lesson 8

Sympathy, Knowledge, and Poise

Sympathy, Knowledge, and Poise seem to be the three ingredients that are most needed in forming the Gentle Person. I place these elements according to their value. No one is great who does not have Sympathy plus, and the greatness of people can be safely gauged by their sympathies.

Sympathy and imagination are twin sisters. Your heart must go out to all people, the high, the low, the rich, the poor, the learned, the unlearned, the good, the bad, the wise and the foolish—it is necessary to be one with them all, else you can never comprehend them. Sympathy! It is the touchstone to every secret, the key to all knowledge, the open sesame of all hearts. Put yourself in the other person's place and then you will know why they think certain things and do certain deeds. Put yourself in their place and your blame will dissolve itself into pity, and your tears will wipe out the record of their misdeeds. The saviors of the world have simply been people with wondrous sympathy.

But Knowledge must go with Sympathy, else the emotions will become maudlin and pity may be wasted on a poodle instead of a child; on a field-mouse instead of a human soul. Knowledge in use is wisdom, and wisdom implies a sense of values—you know a big thing from a little one, a valuable fact from a trivial one. Tragedy and comedy are simply questions of value: a little misfit in life makes us laugh, a great one is tragedy and cause for expression of grief.

Poise is the strength of body and strength of mind to control your Sympathy and your Knowledge. Unless you control your emotions they run over and you stand in the mire. Sympathy must not run riot, or it is valueless and tokens weakness instead of strength. In every hospital for nervous disorders are to be found many instances of this loss of control. The individual has Sympathy but not Poise, and therefore their life is worthless to them and to the world. They symbolize inefficiency and not helpfulness.

Poise reveals itself more in voice than it does in words; more in thought than in action; more in atmosphere than in conscious life. It is a spiritual quality, and is felt more than it is seen. It is not a matter of bodily size, nor of bodily attitude, nor attire, nor of personal comeliness—it is a state of inward being, and of knowing your cause is just. And so you see it is a great and profound subject after all, great in its ramifications, limitless in extent, implying the entire science of right living. I once met a man who was deformed in body and little more than a dwarf, but who had such Spiritual Gravity—such Poise—that to enter a room where he was, was to feel his presence and acknowledge his superiority. To allow Sympathy to waste itself on unworthy objects is to deplete one's life forces. To conserve is the part of wisdom, and reserve is a necessary element in all good literature, as well as in everything else.

Poise being the control of our Sympathy and Knowledge, it implies a possession of these attributes, for without having Sympathy and Knowledge you have nothing to control but your physical body. To practice Poise as a mere gymnastic exercise, or study in etiquette, is to be self-conscious, stiff, preposterous, and ridiculous. Those who cut such fantastic tricks before high heaven as make angels weep are people void of Sympathy and Knowledge trying to cultivate Poise. Their science is a mere matter of what to do with arms and legs. Poise is a question of spirit controlling flesh, heart controlling attitude.

Get Knowledge by coming close to Nature. That person is the greatest who best serves their kind. Sympathy and Knowledge are for use—you acquire that you may give out; you accumulate that you may bestow. And as God has given unto you the sublime blessings of Sympathy and Knowledge, there will come to you the wish to reveal your gratitude by giving them out again; for the wise person is aware that we retain spiritual qualities only as we give them away.

Let your light shine. To him that hath shall be given. The exercise of wisdom brings wisdom; and at the last the infinitesimal quantity of human knowledge, compared with the Infinite, and the smallness of human Sympathy when compared with the source from which ours is absorbed, will evolve an abnegation and a humility that will lend a perfect Poise. The Gentleman is one with perfect Sympathy, Knowledge, and Poise.

Lesson 9

Love and Faith

No woman is worthy to be a wife who on the day of her marriage is not lost absolutely and entirely in an atmosphere of love and perfect trust; the supreme sacredness of the relation is the only thing which, at the time, should possess her soul. Is she a bawd that she should bargain?

Women should not "obey" men any more than men should obey women. There are six requisites in every happy marriage; the first is Faith, and the remaining five are Confidence. Nothing so compliments a man as for a woman to believe in him–nothing so pleases a woman as for a man to place confidence in her.

Obey? God help me! Yes, if I loved a woman, my whole heart's desire would be to obey her slightest wish. And how could I love her unless I had perfect confidence that she would only aspire to what was beautiful, true, and right?

And to enable her to realize this ideal, her wish would be to me a sacred command; and her attitude of mind toward me I know would be the same. And the only rivalry between us would be as to who could love the most; and the desire to obey would be the one controlling impulse of our lives.

We gain freedom by giving it, and he who bestows faith gets it back with interest. To bargain and stipulate in love is to lose.

The woman who stops the marriage ceremony and requests the minister to omit the word "obey" is sowing the first seed of doubt and distrust that later may come to fruition in the divorce court.

The haggling and bickerings of settlements and dowries that usually precede the marriage of "blood" and "dollars" are the unheeded warnings that misery, heartache, suffering, and disgrace await the principals.

Perfect faith implies perfect love, and perfect love casteth out fear. It is always the fear of imposition, and a lurking intent to rule, that causes the woman to haggle over a word—it is absence of love, a limitation, an incapacity. The price of a perfect love is an absolute and complete surrender.

Keep back part of the price and yours will be the fate of Ananias and Sapphira. Your doom is swift and sure. To win all we must give all.

Lesson 10

Giving Something for Nothing

To give a person something for nothing tends to make the individual dissatisfied with themselves. Your enemies are the ones you have helped. And when an individual is dissatisfied with themselves they are dissatisfied with the whole world—and with you.

A person's quarrel with the world is only a quarrel with themselves. But so strong is this inclination to lay blame elsewhere and take credit to ourselves that when we are unhappy we say it is the fault of this woman or that man. Especially do women attribute their misery to That Man.

And often the trouble is he has given her too much for nothing.

This truth is a reversible, back-action one, well lubricated by use, working both ways—as the case may be.

Nobody but a beggar has really definite ideas concerning his rights. People who give much—who love much—do not haggle.

That form of affection which drives sharp bargains and makes demands gets a check on the bank in which there is no balance.

There is nothing so costly as something you get for nothing.

My friend Tom Lowry, Magnate in Ordinary of Minneapolis and the east side of Wall Street, has recently had a little experience that proves my point.

A sturdy beggar-man, a specimen of decayed gentility, once called on Tammas with a hard-luck story and a family Bible, and asked for a small loan on the Good Book.

To be compelled to soak the family Bible would surely melt the heart of stone!

Tom was melted.

Tom made the loan but refused the collateral, stating he had no use for it.

Which was God's truth for once.

In a few weeks the man came back, and tried to tell Tom his hard-luck story concerning the Cold Ingratitude of a Cruel World.

Tom said, "Spare me the slow music and the recital—I have troubles of my own. I need mirth and good cheer—take this dollar, and peace be with you."

"Peace be multiplied unto thee," said the beggar, and departed. The next month the man returned, and began to tell Tom a tale of Cruelty, Injustice, and Ingratitude.

Tom was riled—he had his magnate business to attend to, and he made a remark in italics. The beggar said, "Mr. Lowry, if you had your business a little better systematized, I would not have to trouble you personally—why don't you just speak to your cashier?" And the great man, who once took a party of friends out for a tally-ho ride, and through mental habit collected five cents from each guest, was so pleased at the thought of relief that he pressed the buzzer. The cashier came, and Tom said, "Put this man Grabheimer on your payroll, give him two dollars now and the same the first of every month."

Then turning to the beggar-man, Tom said, "Now get out of here—hurry, vamoose, hike—and be damned to you!"

"The same to you and many of them," said His Effluvia politely, and withdrew.

All this happened two years ago. The beggar got his money regularly for a year, and then in auditing accounts Tom found the name on the payroll, and as Tom could not remember how the name got there, he at first thought the payroll was being stuffed. Anyway he ordered the beggar's name stricken off the roster, and the elevator man was instructed to enforce the edict against beggars.

Not being allowed to see his man, the beggar wrote him letters—denunciatory, scandalous, abusive, threatening. Finally the beggar laid the matter before an obese limb o' the Law, Jaggers, of the firm of Jaggers & Jaggers, who took the case on a contingent fee.

The case came to trial, and Jaggers proved his case *se offendendo*—argal: it was shown by the defendant's books that His Bacteria had been on the payroll and his name had been stricken off without suggestion, request, cause, reason, or fault of his own.

His Crabship proved the contract, and Tom got it in the mazzard. Judgment for plaintiff, with costs. The beggar got the money and Minneapolis Tom got the experience. Tom said the man would lose the money, but he himself has gotten the part that will be his for ninety-nine years. Surely the spirit of justice does not sleep and there is a beneficent and wise Providence that watches over magnates.

Lesson 11

Work and Waste

These truths I hold to be self-evident: That man was made to be happy; that happiness is only attainable through useful effort; that the very best way to help ourselves is to help others, and often the best way to help others is to mind our own business; that useful effort means the proper exercise of all our faculties; that we grow only through exercise; that education should continue through life, and the joys of mental endeavor should be, especially, the solace of the old; that where people alternate work, play, and study in right proportion, the organs of the mind are the last to fail, and death for such has no terrors.

That the possession of wealth can never make a person exempt from useful manual labor; that if all would work a little, no one would then be overworked; that if no one wasted, all would have enough; that if none were overfed, none would be underfed; that the rich and "educated" need education quite as much as the poor and illiterate; that the presence of a serving class is an indictment and a disgrace to our civilization; that the disadvantage of having a serving class falls most upon those who are served, and not upon those who serve—just as the real curse of slavery fell upon the slave-owners.

That people who are waited on by a serving class cannot have a right consideration for the rights of others, and they waste both time and substance, both of which are lost forever, and can only seemingly be made good by additional human effort.

That the person who lives on the labor of others, not giving himself in return to the best of his ability, is really a consumer of human life and therefore must be considered no better than a cannibal.

That each one living naturally will do the thing he can do best, but that in useful service there is no high nor low.

That to set apart one day in seven as "holy" is really absurd and serves only to loosen our grasp on the tangible present.

That all duties, offices, and things which are useful and necessary to humanity are sacred, and that nothing else is or can be sacred.

Lesson 12

The Law of Obedience

The very first item in the creed of common sense is *Obedience*. Perform your work with a whole heart.

Revolt may be sometimes necessary, but the person who tries to mix revolt and obedience is doomed to disappoint themselves and everybody with whom they have dealings. To flavor work with protest is to fail absolutely.

When you revolt, why, revolt–climb, hike, get out, defy–tell everybody and everything to go to hades! That disposes of the case. You thus separate yourself entirely from those you have served–no one misunderstands you–you have declared yourself.

The person who quits in disgust when ordered to perform a task which they consider menial or unjust may be a pretty good person, but in the wrong environment; but the malcontent who takes your order with a smile and then secretly disobeys is a dangerous proposition. To pretend to obey, and yet carry in your heart the spirit of revolt is to do half-hearted, slipshod work. If revolt and obedience are equal in power, your engine will then stop on the center and you benefit no one, not even yourself.

The spirit of obedience is the controlling impulse that dominates the receptive mind and the hospitable heart. There are boats that mind the helm and there are boats that do not. Those that do not get holes knocked in them sooner or later.

To keep off the rocks, obey the rudder.

Obedience is not to slavishly obey this person or that, but it is that cheerful mental state which responds to the necessity of the case, and does the thing without any back talk–unuttered or expressed.

Obedience to the institution–loyalty! The one who has not learned to obey has trouble ahead of them every step of the way. The world has it in for them continually, because they have it in for the world.

The one who does not know how to receive orders is not fit to issue them to others. But the individual who knows how to execute the orders given them is preparing the way to issue orders, and better still–to have them obeyed.

From <u>Garcia</u> to The <u>Go-Getter</u>

Rowan was a man who carried out an impossible mission because he believed in duty over discussion.

Next, you'll meet Bill Peck—a fictional character with very real traits. Like Rowan, Peck is given a job that seems simple but turns out to be a maze of obstacles. What makes this story remarkable isn't just how hard the job is—it's how determined Peck is to *not* be deterred. He doesn't complain. He doesn't ask for help. He doesn't even think of quitting. He just *makes it happen.*

Rowan and Peck never met, but they were cut from the same cloth. They understood the value of personal responsibility. They lived by a code: take action, get the job done, no matter what.

Let *The Go-Getter* remind you: It's not about what stands in your way—it's about how badly you want to finish the mission.

The Go-Getter
A Story That Tells You How to Be One

PETER B. KYNE

Peter B. Kyne's Dedication

This little book is dedicated to the memory of my dead chief, Brigadier-General Leroy S. Lyon, sometime commander of the 65th Field Artillery Brigade, 40th Division, United States Army.

He practiced and preached a religion of loyalty to the country and the appointed task, whatever it might be.

Chapter I

Mr. Alden P. Ricks, known in Pacific Coast wholesale lumber and shipping circles as Cappy Ricks, had more troubles than a hen with ducklings. He remarked as much to Mr. Skinner, president and general manager of the Ricks Logging & Lumbering Company, the corporate entity which represented Cappy's vast lumber interests; and he fairly barked the information at Captain Matt Peasley, his son-in-law and also president and manager of the Blue Star Navigation Company, another corporate entity which represented the Ricks interest in the American mercantile marine.

Mr. Skinner received this information in silence. He was not related to Cappy Ricks. But Matt Peasley sat down, crossed his legs and matched glares with his mercurial father-in-law.

"*You* have troubles!" he jeered, with emphasis on the pronoun. "Have you got a misery in your back, or is Herbert Hoover the wrong man for Secretary of Commerce?"

"Stow your sarcasm, young feller," Cappy shrilled. "You know dad-blamed well it isn't a question of health or politics. It's the fact that in my old age I find myself totally surrounded by the choicest aggregation of mental duds since Ajax defied the lightning."

"Meaning whom?"

"You and Skinner."

"Why, what have we done?"

"You argued me into taking on the management of twenty-five of those infernal Shipping Board freighters, and no sooner do we have them allocated to us than a near panic hits the country, freight rates go to glory, marine engineers go on strike and every infernal young whelp we send out to take charge of one of our offices in the Orient promptly gets the swelled head and thinks he's divinely ordained to drink up all the synthetic Scotch whiskey manufactured in Japan for the benefit of thirsty Americans. In my old age you two have forced us into the position of having to fire folks by cable. Why? Because we're breaking into a game that can't be played on the home grounds. A lot of our business is so far away we can't control it."

Matt Peasley leveled an accusing finger at Cappy Ricks. "We never argued you into taking over the management of those Shipping Board boats. We argued me into it. I'm the goat. You have nothing to do with it. You retired ten years ago. All the troubles in the marine end of this shop belong on my capable shoulders, old settler."

"Theoretically–yes. Actually–no. I hope you do not expect me to abandon mental as well as physical effort. Great Wampus Cats! Am I to be denied a sentimental interest in matters where I have a controlling financial interest?

I admit you two boys are running my affairs and ordinarily you run them rather well, but—but—ahem! Harumph-h-h! What's the matter with you, Matt? And you, also, Skinner? If Matt makes a mistake, it's your job to remind him of it before the results manifest themselves, is it not? And vice versa. Have you two boobs lost your ability to judge men or did you ever have such ability?"

"You're referring to Henderson, of the Shanghai office, I dare say," Mr. Skinner cut in.

"I am, Skinner. And I'm here to remind you that if we'd stuck to our own game, which is coast-wise shipping, and had left the trans-Pacific field with its general cargoes to others, we wouldn't have any Shanghai office at this moment and we would not be pestered by the Hendersons of this world."

"He's the best lumber salesman we've ever had," Mr. Skinner defended. "I had every hope that he would send us orders for many a cargo for Asiatic delivery."

"And he had gone through every job in this office, from office boy to sales manager in the lumber department and from freight clerk to passenger agent in the navigation company," Matt Peasley supplemented.

"I admit all of that. But did you consult me when you decided to send him out to China on his own?"

"Of course not. I'm boss of the Blue Star Navigation Company, am I not? The man was in charge of the Shanghai office before you ever opened your mouth to discharge your cargo of free advice."

"I told you then that Henderson wouldn't make good, didn't I?"

"You did."

"And now I have an opportunity to tell you the little tale you didn't give me an opportunity to tell you before you sent him out. Henderson *was* a good man—a crackerjack man—when he had a better man over him. But—I've been twenty years reducing a tendency on the part of that fellow's head to bust his hat-band. And now he's gone south with a hundred and thirty thousand taels of our Shanghai bank account."

"Permit me to remind you, Mr. Ricks," Mr. Skinner cut in coldly, "that he was bonded to the extent of a quarter of a million dollars."

"Not a peep out of you, Skinner. Not a peep. Permit me to remind *you* that I'm the little genius who placed that insurance unknown to you and Matt. And I recall now that I was reminded by you, Matthew, my son, that I had retired ten years ago and please, would I quit interfering in the internal administration of your office."

"Well, I must admit your far-sightedness in that instance will keep the Shanghai office out of the red ink this year," Matt Peasley replied. "However, we face this situation, Cappy. Henderson has drunk and gambled and signed chits in excess of his salary. He hasn't attended to business and he's capped his inefficiency by absconding with our bank account. We couldn't foresee that. When we send a man out to the Orient to be our manager there, we have to trust him all the way or not at all. So there is no use weeping over spilled milk, Cappy. Our job is to select a successor to Henderson and send him out to Shanghai on the next boat."

"Oh, very well, Matt," Cappy replied magnanimously, "I'll not rub it into you. I suppose I'm far from generous, bawling you out like this. Perhaps, when you're my age and have a lot of mental and moral cripples nip you and draw blood as often as they've drawn it on me you'll be a better judge than I of men worthy of the weight of responsibility. Skinner, have you got a candidate for this job?"

"I regret to say, sir, I have not. All of the men in my department are quite young—too young for the responsibility."

"What do you mean—young?" Cappy blazed.

"Well, the only man I would consider for the job is Andrews and he is too young—about thirty, I should say."

"About thirty, eh? Strikes me you were about twenty-eight when I threw ten thousand a year at you in actual cash, and a couple of million dollars' worth of responsibility."

"Yes sir, but then Andrews has never been tested—"

"Skinner," Cappy interrupted in his most awful voice, "it's a constant source of amazement to me why I refrain from firing you. You say Andrews has never been tested.

Why hasn't he been tested? Why are we maintaining untested material in this shop, anyhow? Eh? Answer me that. Tut, tut, tut! Not a peep out of you, sir. If you had done your Christian duty, you would have taken a year's vacation when lumber was selling itself in 1919 and 1920, and you would have left Andrews sitting in at your desk to see the sort of stuff he's made of."

"It's a mighty lucky thing I didn't go away for a year," Skinner protested respectfully, "because the market broke—like that—and if you don't think we have to hustle to sell sufficient lumber to keep our own ships busy freighting it—"

"Skinner, how dare you contradict me? How old was Matt Peasley when I turned over the Blue Star Navigation Company to him, lock, stock and barrel? Why, he wasn't twenty-six years old. Skinner, you're a dodo! The killjoys like you who have straddled the neck of industry and throttled it with absurd theories that a man's back must be bent like an ox-bow and his locks snowy white before he can be entrusted with responsibility and a living wage, have caused all of our wars and strikes. This is a young man's world, Skinner, and don't you ever forget it. The go-getters of this world are under thirty years of age. Matt," he concluded, turning to his son-in-law, "what do you think of Andrews for that Shanghai job?"

"I think he'll do."

"Why do you think he'll do?"

"Because he ought to do. He's been with us long enough to have acquired sufficient experience to enable him—"

"Has he acquired the courage to tackle the job, Matt?" Cappy interrupted. "That's more important than this doggoned experience you and Skinner prate so much about."

"I know nothing of his courage. I assume that he has force and initiative. I know he has a pleasing personality."

"Well, before we send him out we ought to know whether or no he has force and initiative."

"Then," quoth Matt Peasley, rising, "I wash my hands of the job of selecting Henderson's successor. You've butted in, so I suggest you name the lucky man."

"Yes, indeed," Skinner agreed. "I'm sure it's quite beyond my poor abilities to uncover Andrews' force and initiative on such notice. He does possess sufficient force and initiative for his present job, but—"

"But will he possess force and initiative when he has to make a quick decision six thousand miles from expert advice, and stand or fall by that decision? That's what we want to know, Skinner."

"I suggest, sir," Mr. Skinner replied with chill politeness, "that you conduct the examination."

"I accept the nomination, Skinner. By the Holy Pink-toed Prophet! The next man we send out to that Shanghai office is going to be a go-getter. We've had three managers go rotten on us and that's three too many."

And without further ado, Cappy swung his aged legs up on to his desk and slid down in his swivel chair until he rested on his spine. His head sank on his breast and he closed his eyes.

"He's framing the examination for Andrews," Matt Peasley whispered, as he and Skinner made their exits.

Chapter II

The President emeritus of the Ricks' interests was not destined to uninterrupted cogitation, however. Within ten minutes his private exchange operator called him to the telephone.

"What is it?" Cappy yelled into the transmitter.

"There is a young man in the general office. His name is Mr. William E. Peck and he desires to see you personally."

Cappy sighed. "Very well," he replied. "Have him shown in."

Almost immediately the office boy ushered Mr. Peck into Cappy's presence. The moment he was fairly inside the door the visitor halted, came easily and naturally to "attention" and bowed respectfully, while the cool glance of his keen blue eyes held steadily the autocrat of the Blue Star Navigation Company.

"Mr. Ricks, Peck is my name, sir—William E. Peck. Thank you, sir, for acceding to my request for an interview."

"Ahem! Hum-m-m!" Cappy looked belligerent. "Sit down, Mr. Peck."

Mr. Peck sat down, but as he crossed to the chair beside Cappy's desk, the old gentleman noticed that his visitor walked with a slight limp, and that his left forearm had been amputated half way to the elbow. To the observant Cappy, the American Legion button in Mr. Peck's lapel told the story.

"Well, Mr. Peck," he queried gently, "what can I do for you?"

"I've called for my job," the veteran replied briefly.

"By the Holy Pink-toed Prophet!" Cappy ejaculated, "you say that like a man who doesn't expect to be refused."

"Quite right, sir. I do not anticipate a refusal."

"Why?"

Mr. William E. Peck's engaging but somewhat plain features rippled into the most compelling smile Cappy Ricks had ever seen. "I am a salesman, Mr. Ricks," he replied. "I know that statement to be true because I have demonstrated, over a period of five years, that I can sell my share of anything that has a hockable value. I have always found, however, that before proceeding to sell goods I had to sell the manufacturer of those goods something, to-wit–myself! I am about to sell myself to you."

"Son," said Cappy smilingly, "you win. You've sold me already. When did they sell you a membership in the military forces of the United States of America?"

"On the morning of April 7th, 1917, sir."

"That clinches our sale. I soldiered with the Knights of Columbus at Camp Kearny myself, but when they refused to let me go abroad with my division my heart was broken, so I went over the hill."

That little touch of the language of the line appeared to warm Mr. Peck's heart considerably, establishing at once a free masonry between them.

"I was with the Portland Lumber Company, selling lumber in the Middle West before the war," he explained. "Uncle Sam gave me my sheepskin at Letter-man General Hospital last week, with half disability on my ten thousand dollars' worth of government insurance. Whittling my wing was a mere trifle, but my broken leg was a long time mending, and now it's shorter than it really ought to be. And I developed pneumonia with influenza and they found some T.B. indications after that. I've been at the government tuberculosis hospital at Fort Bayard, New Mexico, for a year. However, what's left of me is certified to be sound. I've got five inches chest expansion and I feel fine."

"Not at all blue or discouraged?" Cappy hazarded.

"Oh, I got off easy, Mr. Ricks. I have my head left—and my right arm. I can think and I can write, and even if one of my wheels is flat, I can hike longer and faster after an order than most. Got a job for me, Mr. Ricks?"

"No, I haven't, Mr. Peck. I'm out of it, you know. Retired ten years ago. This office is merely a headquarters for social frivolity—a place to get my mail and mill over the gossip of the street. Our Mr. Skinner is the chap you should see."

"I have seen Mr. Skinner, sir," the erstwhile warrior replied, "but he wasn't very sympathetic. I think he jumped to the conclusion that I was attempting to trade him my empty sleeve. He informed me that there wasn't sufficient business to keep his present staff of salesmen busy, so then I told him I'd take anything, from stenographer up. I'm the champion one-handed typist of the United States Army. I can tally lumber and bill it. I can keep books and answer the telephone."

"No encouragement, eh?"

"No, sir."

"Well, now, son," Cappy informed his cheerful visitor confidentially, "you take my tip and see my son-in-law, Captain Peasley. He's high, low and jack-in-the-game in the shipping end of our business."

"I have also interviewed Captain Peasley. He was very kind. He said he felt that he owed me a job, but business is so bad he couldn't make a place for me. He told me he is now carrying a dozen ex-service men merely because he hasn't the heart to let them go. I believe him."

"Well, my dear boy—my dear young friend! Why do you come to me?"

"Because," Mr. Peck replied smilingly, "I want you to go over their heads and give me a job. I don't care a hoot what it is, provided I can do it. If I can do it, I'll do it better than it was ever done before, and if I can't do that I'll quit to save you the embarrassment of firing me. I'm not an object of charity, but I'm scarcely the man I used to be and I'm four years behind the procession and have to catch up. I have the best of references—"

"I see you have," Cappy cut in blandly, and pressed the push-button on his desk. Mr. Skinner entered. He glanced disapprovingly at William E. Peck and then turned inquiring eyes toward Cappy Ricks.

"Skinner, dear boy," Cappy purred amiably, "I've been thinking over the proposition to send Andrews out to the Shanghai office, and I've come to this conclusion. We'll have to take a chance. At the present time that office is in charge of a stenographer, and we've got to get a manager on the job without further loss of time. So I'll tell you what we'll do. We'll send Andrews out on the next boat, but inform him that his position is temporary. Then if he doesn't make good out there we can take him back into this office, where he is a most valuable man. Meanwhile—ahem! hum-m-m! Harumph!—meanwhile, you'd oblige me greatly, Skinner, my dear boy, if you would consent to take this young man into your office and give him a good work-out to see the stuff he's made of. As a favor to me, Skinner, my dear boy, as a favor to me."

Mr. Skinner, in the language of the sporting world, was down for the count—and knew it. Young Mr. Peck knew it too, and smiled graciously upon the general manager, for young Mr. Peck had been in the army, where one of the first great lessons to be assimilated is this: that the commanding general's request is always tantamount to an order.

"Very well, sir," Mr. Skinner replied coldly. "Have you arranged the compensation to be given Mr. Peck?"

Cappy threw up a deprecating hand. "That detail is entirely up to you, Skinner. Far be it from me to interfere in the internal administration of your department. Naturally you will pay Mr. Peck what he is worth and not a cent more." He turned to the triumphant Peck. "Now, you listen to me, young feller. If you think you're slipping gracefully into a good thing, disabuse your mind of that impression right now. You'll step right up to the plate, my son, and you'll hit the ball fairly on the nose, and you'll do it early and often. The first time you tip a foul, you'll be warned. The second time you do it you'll get a month's lay-off to think it over, and the third time you'll be out—for keeps. Do I make myself clear?"

"You do, sir," Mr. Peck declared happily. "All I ask is fighting room and I'll hack my way into Mr. Skinner's heart. Thank you, Mr. Skinner, for consenting to take me on. I appreciate your action very, very much and shall endeavor to be worthy of your confidence."

"Young scoundrel! In-fer-nal young scoundrel!" Cappy murmured to himself. "He has a sense of humor, thank God! Ah, poor old narrow-gauge Skinner! If that fellow ever gets a new or unconventional thought in his stodgy head, it'll kill him overnight. He's hopping mad right now, because he can't say a word in his own defense, but if he doesn't make hell look like a summer holiday for Mr. Bill Peck, I'm due to be mercifully chloroformed. Good Lord, how empty life would be if I couldn't butt in and raise a little riot every once in so often."

Young Mr. Peck had risen and was standing at attention. "When do I report for duty, sir?" he queried of Mr. Skinner.

"Whenever you're ready," Skinner retorted with a wintry smile. Mr. Peck glanced at a cheap wrist watch. "It's twelve o'clock now," he soliloquized aloud. "I'll pop out, wrap myself around some rations and report on the job at one P.M. I might just as well knock out half a day's pay." He glanced at Cappy Ricks and quoted:

"Count that day lost whose low descending sun

Finds prices shot to glory and business done for fun."

Unable to maintain his composure in the face of such levity during office hours, Mr. Skinner withdrew, still wrapped in his sub-Antarctic dignity. As the door closed behind him, Mr. Peck's eyebrows went up in a manner indicative of apprehension.

"I'm off to a bad start, Mr. Ricks," he opined.

"You only asked for a start," Cappy piped back at him. "I didn't guarantee you a *good* start, and I wouldn't because I can't. I can only drive Skinner and Matt Peasley so far—and no farther. There's always a point at which I quit—er—ah—William."

"More familiarly known as Bill Peck, sir."

"Very well, Bill." Cappy slid out to the edge of his chair and peered at Bill Peck balefully over the top of his spectacles. "I'll have my eye on you, young feller," he shrilled. "I freely acknowledge our indebtedness to you, but the day you get the notion in your head that this office is an old soldiers' home—" He paused thoughtfully. "I wonder what Skinner *will* pay you?" he mused. "Oh, well," he continued, whatever it is, take it and say nothing and when the moment is propitious—and provided you've earned it—I'll intercede with the danged old relic and get you a raise."

"Thank you very much, sir. You are most kind. Good-day, sir."

And Bill Peck picked up his hat and limped out of The Presence. Scarcely had the door closed behind him than Mr. Skinner re-entered Cappy Ricks' lair. He opened his mouth to speak, but Cappy silenced him with an imperious finger.

"Not a peep out of you, Skinner, my dear boy," he chirped amiably. "I know exactly what you're going to say and I admit your right to say it, but—as—ahem! Harumph-h-h! Now, Skinner, listen to reason. How the devil could you have the heart to reject that crippled ex-soldier? There he stood, on one sound leg, with his sleeve tucked into his coat pocket and on his homely face the grin of an unwhipped, unbeatable man. But you—blast your cold, unfeeling soul, Skinner!—looked him in the eye and turned him down like a drunkard turns down near-beer. Skinner, how *could* you do it?"

Undaunted by Cappy's admonitory finger, Mr. Skinner struck a distinctly defiant attitude.

"There is no sentiment in business," he replied angrily. "A week ago last Thursday the local posts of the American Legion commenced their organized drive for jobs for their crippled and unemployed comrades, and within three days you've sawed off two hundred and nine such jobs on the various corporations that you control. The gang you shipped up to the mill in Washington has already applied for a charter for a new post to be known as Cappy Ricks Post No. 534. And you had experienced men discharged to make room for these ex-soldiers."

"You bet I did," Cappy yelled triumphantly. "It's always Old Home Week in every logging camp and saw-mill in the Northwest for IWW's and revolutionary communists. I'm sick of their unauthorized strikes and sabotage, and by the Holy Pink-Toed Prophet, Cappy Ricks Post. No. 534, American Legion, is the only sort of back-fire I can think of to put the Wobblies on the run."

"Every office and ship and retail yard could be run by a first-sergeant," Skinner complained. "I'm thinking of having reveille and retreat and bugle calls and Saturday morning inspections. I tell you, sir, the Ricks interests have absorbed all the old soldiers possible and at the present moment those interests are overflowing with glory. What we want are workers, not talkers. These ex-soldiers spend too much time fighting their battles over again."

"Well, Comrade Peck is the last one I'll ask you to absorb, Skinner," Cappy promised contritely. "Ever read Kipling's *Barrack Room Ballads*, Skinner?"

"I have no time to read," Mr. Skinner protested.

"Go up town this minute and buy a copy and read one ballad entitled 'Tommy,'" Cappy barked. "For the good of your immortal soul," he added.

"Well, Comrade Peck doesn't make a hit with me, Mr. Ricks. He applied to me for a job and I gave him his answer. Then he went to Captain Matt and was refused, so, just to demonstrate his bad taste, he went over our heads and induced you to pitchfork him into a job. He'll curse the day he was inspired to do that."

"Skinner! Skinner! Look me in the eye! Do you know why I asked you to take on Bill Peck?"

"I do. Because you're too tender-hearted for your own good."

"You unimaginative dunderhead! You jibbering jackdaw! How could I reject a boy who simply would not be rejected? Why, I'll bet a ripe peach that Bill Peck was one of the doggondest finest soldiers you ever saw. He carries his objective. He sized you up just like that, Skinner. He declined to permit you to block him. Skinner, that Peck person has been opposed by experts. Yes, sir—experts! What kind of a job are you going to give him, Skinner, my dear boy?"

"Andrews' job, of course."

"Oh, yes, I forgot. Skinner, dear boy, haven't we got about half a million feet of skunk spruce to saw off on somebody?" Mr. Skinner nodded and Cappy continued with all the naïve eagerness of one who has just made a marvelous discovery, which he is confident will revolutionize science. "Give him that stinking stuff to peddle, Skinner, and if you can dig up a couple of dozen carloads of red fir or bull pine in transit, or some short or odd-length stock, or some larch ceiling or flooring, or some hemlock random stock—in fact, anything the trade doesn't want as a gift—you get me, don't you, Skinner?"

Mr. Skinner smiled his swordfish smile. "And if he fails to make good—*au revoir*, eh?"

"Yes, I suppose so, although I hate to think about it. On the other hand, if he makes good he's to have Andrews' salary. We must be fair, Skinner. Whatever our faults we must always be fair." He rose and patted the general manager's lean shoulder. "There, there, Skinner, my boy. Forgive me if I've been a trifle—ah—ahem!—precipitate and—er—harumph-h-h! Skinner, if you put a prohibitive price on that skunk fir, by the Holy Pink-toed Prophet, I'll fire you! Be fair, boy, be fair. No dirty work, Skinner. Remember, Comrade Peck has half of his left forearm buried in France."

Chapter III

At twelve-thirty, as Cappy was hurrying up California Street to luncheon at the Commercial Club, he met Bill Peck limping down the sidewalk. The ex-soldier stopped him and handed him a card.

"What do you think of that, sir?" he queried. "Isn't it a neat business card?"

Cappy read:

RICKS LUMBER & LOGGING COMPANY
Lumber and its products
248 California St.
San Francisco.
Represented by
William E. Peck
If you can drive nails in it—we have it!

Cappy Ricks ran a speculative thumb over Comrade Peck's business card. It was engraved. And copper plates or steel dies are not made in half an hour!

"By the Twelve Ragged Apostles!" This was Cappy's most terrible oath and he never employed it unless rocked to his very foundations. "Bill, as one bandit to another—come clean. When did you first make up your mind to go to work for us?"

"A week ago," Comrade Peck replied blandly.

"And what was your grade when Kaiser Bill went AWOL?"

"I was a buck."

"I don't believe you. Didn't anybody ever offer you something better?"

"Frequently. However, if I had accepted I would have had to resign the nicest job I ever had. There wasn't much money in it, but it was filled with excitement and interesting experiments. I used to disguise myself as a Christmas tree or a box car and pick off German sharp-shooters. I was known as Peck's Bad Boy. I was often tempted to quit, but whenever I'd reflect on the number of American lives I was saving daily, a commission was just a scrap of paper to me."

"If you'd ever started in any other branch of the service you'd have run John J. Pershing down to lance corporal. Bill, listen! Have you ever had any experience selling skunk spruce?"

Comrade Peck was plainly puzzled. He shook his head. "What sort of stock is it?" he asked.

"Humboldt County, California, spruce, and it's coarse and stringy and wet and heavy and smells just like a skunk directly after using. I'm afraid Skinner's going to start you at the bottom—and skunk spruce is it.

"Can you drive nails in it, Mr. Ricks?"

"Oh, yes."

"Does anybody ever buy skunk spruce, sir?"

"Oh, occasionally one of our bright young men digs up a half-wit who's willing to try anything once. Otherwise, of course, we would not continue to manufacture it. Fortunately, Bill, we have very little of it, but whenever our woods boss runs across a good tree he hasn't the heart to leave it standing, and as a result, we always have enough skunk spruce on hand to keep our salesmen humble."

"I can sell anything—at a price," Comrade Peck replied unconcernedly, and continued on his way back to the office.

Chapter IV

For two months Cappy Ricks saw nothing of Bill Peck. That enterprising veteran had been sent out into the Utah, Arizona, New Mexico and Texas territory the moment he had familiarized himself with the numerous details regarding freight rates, weights and the mills he represented, all things which a salesman should be familiar with before he starts out on the road. From Salt Lake City he wired an order for two carloads of larch rustic and in Ogden he managed to inveigle a retail yard with which Mr. Skinner had been trying to do business for years, into sampling a carload of skunk spruce boards, random lengths and grades, at a dollar above the price given him by Skinner. In Arizona he worked up some new business in mining timbers, but it was not until he got into the heart of Texas that Comrade Peck really commenced to demonstrate his selling ability. Standard oil derricks were his specialty and he shot the orders in so fast that Mr. Skinner was forced to wire him for mercy and instruct him to devote his talent to the disposal of cedar shingles and siding, Douglas fir and redwood. Eventually he completed his circle and worked his way home, via Los Angeles, pausing however, in the San Joaquin Valley to sell two more carloads of skunk spruce.

When this order was wired in, Mr. Skinner came to Cappy Ricks with the telegram.

"Well, I must admit Comrade Peck can sell lumber," he announced grudgingly. "He has secured five new accounts and here is an order for two more carloads of skunk spruce. I'll have to raise his salary about the first of the year.

"My dear Skinner, why the devil wait until the first of the year? Your pernicious habit of deferring the inevitable parting with money has cost us the services of more than one good man. You know you have to raise Comrade Peck's salary sooner or later, so why not do it now and smile like a dentifrice advertisement while you're doing it? Comrade Peck will feel a whole lot better as a result, and who knows? He may conclude you're a human being, after all, and learn to love you?"

"Very well, sir. I'll give him the same salary Andrews was getting before Peck took over his territory."

"Skinner, you make it impossible for me to refrain from showing you who's boss around here. He's better than Andrews, isn't he?"

"I think he is, sir."

"Well then, for the love of a square deal, pay him more and pay it to him from the first day he went to work. Get out. You make me nervous. By the way, how is Andrews getting along in his Shanghai job?"

"He's helping the cable company pay its income tax. Cables about three times a week on matters he should decide for himself. Matt Peasley is disgusted with him."

"Ah! Well, I'm not disappointed. And I suppose Matt will be in here before long to remind me that I was the bright boy who picked Andrews for the job. Well, I did, but I call upon you to remember, Skinner, when I'm assailed, that Andrews' appointment was temporary."

"Yes, sir, it was."

"Well, I suppose I'll have to cast about for his successor and beat Matt out of his cheap 'I told you so' triumph. I think Comrade Peck has some of the earmarks of a good manager for our Shanghai office, but I'll have to test him a little further." He looked up humorously at Mr. Skinner. "Skinner, my dear boy," he continued, "I'm going to have him deliver a blue vase."

Mr. Skinner's cold features actually glowed. "Well, tip the chief of police and the proprietor of the store off this time and save yourself some money," he warned Cappy. He walked to the window and looked down into California Street. He continued to smile.

"Yes," Cappy continued dreamily, "I think I shall give him the thirty-third degree. You'll agree with me, Skinner, that if he delivers the blue vase he'll be worth ten thousand dollars a year as our Oriental manager?"

"I'll say he will," Mr. Skinner replied slangily.

"Very well, then. Arrange matters, Skinner, so that he will be available for me at one o'clock, a week from Sunday. I'll attend to the other details."

Mr. Skinner nodded. He was still chuckling when he departed for his own office.

Chapter V

A week from the succeeding Saturday, Mr. Skinner did not come down to the office, but a telephone message from his home informed the chief clerk that Mr. Skinner was at home and somewhat indisposed. The chief clerk was to advise Mr. Peck that he, Mr. Skinner, had contemplated having a conference with the latter that day, but that his indisposition would prevent this. Mr. Skinner hoped to be feeling much better tomorrow, and since he was very desirous of a conference with Mr. Peck before the latter should depart on his next selling pilgrimage, on Monday, would Mr. Peck be good enough to call at Mr. Skinner's house at one o'clock Sunday afternoon? Mr. Peck sent back word that he would be there at the appointed time and was rewarded with Mr. Skinner's thanks, via the chief clerk.

Promptly at one o'clock the following day, Bill Peck reported at the general manager's house. He found Mr. Skinner in bed, reading the paper and looking surprisingly well. He trusted Mr. Skinner felt better than he looked. Mr. Skinner did, and at once entered into a discussion of the new customers, other prospects he particularly desired Mr. Peck to approach, new business to be investigated, and further details without end. And in the midst of this conference Cappy Riggs telephoned.

A portable telephone stood on a commode beside Mr. Skinner's bed, so the latter answered immediately. Comrade Peck watched Skinner listen attentively for fully two minutes, then heard him say:

"Mr. Ricks, I'm terribly sorry. I'd love to do this errand for you, but really I'm under the weather. In fact, I'm in bed as I speak to you now. But Mr. Peck is here with me and I'm sure he'll be very happy to attend to the matter for you."

"By all means," Bill Peck hastened to assure the general manager. "Who does Mr. Ricks want killed and where will he have the body delivered?"

"Hah-hah! Hah-hah!" Mr. Skinner had a singularly annoying, mirthless laugh, as if he begrudged himself such an unheard-of indulgence. "Mr. Peck says," he informed Cappy, "that he'll be delighted to attend to the matter for you. He wants to know whom you want killed and where you wish the body delivered. Hah-hah! Hah! Peck, Mr. Ricks will speak to you."

Bill Peck took the telephone. "Good afternoon, Mr. Ricks."

"Hello, old soldier. What are you doing this afternoon?"

"Nothing—after I conclude my conference with Mr. Skinner. By the way, he has just given me a most handsome boost in salary, for which I am most appreciative. I feel, however, despite Mr. Skinner's graciousness, that you have put in a kind word for me with him, and I want to thank you—"

"Tut, tut. Not a peep out of you, sir. Not a peep. You get nothing for nothing from Skinner or me. However, in view of the fact that you're feeling kindly toward me this afternoon, I wish you'd do a little errand for me. I can't send a boy and I hate to make a messenger out of you—er—ah—ahem! That is har-umph-h-h—!"

"I have no false pride, Mr. Ricks."

"Thank you, Bill. Glad you feel that way about it. Bill, I was prowling around town this forenoon, after church, and down in a store on Sutter Street, between Stockton and Powell Street, on the right hand side as you face Market Street, I saw a blue vase in a window. I have a weakness for vases, Bill. I'm a sharp on them, too. Now, this vase I saw isn't very expensive as vases go—in fact, I wouldn't buy it for my collection—but one of the finest and sweetest ladies of my acquaintance has the mate to that blue vase I saw in the window, and I know she'd be prouder than Punch if she had two of them—one for each side of her drawing room mantel, understand?

"Now, I'm leaving from the Southern Pacific depot at eight o'clock tonight, bound for Santa Barbara to attend her wedding anniversary tomorrow night. I forget what anniversary it is, Bill, but I have been informed by my daughter that I'll be very much *de trop* if I send her any present other than something in porcelain or China or Cloisonné—well, Bill, this crazy little blue vase just fills the order. Understand?"

"Yes, sir. You feel that it would be most graceful on your part if you could bring this little blue vase down to Santa Barbara with you tonight. You have to have it tonight, because if you wait until the store opens on Monday the vase will reach your hostess twenty-four hours after her anniversary party."

"Exactly, Bill. Now, I've simply got to have that vase. If I had discovered it yesterday I wouldn't be asking you to get it for me today, Bill."

"Please do not make any explanations or apologies, Mr. Ricks. You have described the vase—no you haven't. What sort of blue is it, how tall is it and what is, approximately, its greatest diameter? Does it set on a base, or does it not? Is it a solid blue, or is it figured?"

It's a Cloisonné vase, Bill—sort of old Dutch blue, or Delft, with some Oriental funny-business on it. I couldn't describe it exactly, but it has some birds and flowers on it. It's about a foot tall and four inches in diameter and sets on a teakwood base."

"Very well, sir. You shall have it."

"And you'll deliver it to me in stateroom A, car 7, aboard the train at Third and Townsend Streets, at seven fifty-five tonight?"

"Yes, sir."

"Thank you, Bill. The expense will be trifling. Collect it from the cashier in the morning, and tell him to charge it to my account." And Cappy hung up.

At once Mr. Skinner took up the thread of the interrupted conference, and it was not until three o'clock that Bill Peck left his house and proceeded downtown to locate Cappy Rick's blue vase.

He proceeded to the block in Sutter Street between Stockton and Powell Streets, and although he walked patiently up one side of the street and down the other, not a single vase of any description showed in any shop window, nor could he find a single shop where such a vase as Cappy had described might, perchance, be displayed for sale.

"I think the old boy has erred in the coordinates of the target," Bill Peck concluded, "or else I misunderstood him. I'll telephone his house and ask him to repeat them."

He did, but nobody was at home except a Swedish maid, and all she knew was that Mr. Ricks was out and the hour of his return was unknown. So Mr. Peck went back to Sutter Street and scoured once more every shop window in the block. Then he scouted two blocks above Powell and two blocks below Stockton. Still the blue vase remained invisible.

So he transferred his search to a corresponding area on Bush Street, and when that failed, he went painstakingly over four blocks of Post Street. He was still without results when he moved one block further west and one further south and discovered the blue vase in a huge plate-glass window of a shop on Geary Street near Grant Avenue. He surveyed it critically and was convinced that it was the object he sought.

He tried the door, but it was locked, as he had anticipated it would be. So he kicked the door and raised an infernal racket, hoping against hope that the noise might bring a watchman from the rear of the building. In vain. He backed out to the edge of the sidewalk and read the sign over the door:

B. Cohen's Art Shop

This was a start, so Mr. Peck limped over to the Palace Hotel and procured a telephone directory. By actual count there were nineteen B. Cohens scattered throughout the city, so before commencing to call the nineteen, Bill Peck borrowed the city directory from the hotel clerk and scanned it for the particular B. Cohen who owned the art shop. His search availed him nothing. B. Cohen was listed as an art dealer at the address where the blue vase reposed in the show window. That was all.

"I suppose he's a commuter," Mr. Peck concluded, and at once proceeded to procure directories of the adjacent cities of Berkeley, Oakland and Alameda. They were not available, so in despair he changed a dollar into five cent pieces, sought a telephone booth and commenced calling up all the B. Cohens in San Francisco. Of the nineteen, four did not answer, three were temporarily disconnected, six replied in Yiddish, five were not the B. Cohen he sought, and one swore he was Irish and that his name was spelled Cohan and pronounced with an accent on both syllables.

The B. Cohens resident in Berkeley, Oakland, Alameda, San Rafael, Sausalito, Mill Valley, San Mateo, Redwood City and Palo Alto were next telephoned to, and when this long and expensive task was done, Ex-Private Bill Peck emerged from the telephone booth wringing wet with perspiration and as irritable as a clucking hen. Once outside the hotel he raised his haggard face to heaven and dumbly queried of the Almighty what He meant by saving him from quick death on the field of honor only to condemn him to be talked to death by B. Cohens in civil life.

It was now six o'clock. Suddenly Peck had an inspiration. Was the name spelled Cohen, Cohan, Cohn, Kohn or Coen?

"If I have to take a Jewish census again tonight I'll die," he told himself desperately, and went back to the art shop.

The sign read:

B. Cohn's Art Shop.

"I wish I knew a bootlegger's joint," poor Peck complained. "I'm pretty far gone and a little wood alcohol couldn't hurt me much now. Why, I could have sworn that name was spelled with an E. It seems to me I noted that particularly."

He went back to the hotel telephone booth and commenced calling up all the B. Cohns in town. There were eight of them and six of them were out, one was maudlin with liquor and the other was very deaf and shouted unintelligibly.

"Peace hath its barbarities no less than war," Mr. Peck sighed. He changed a twenty-dollar bill into nickles, dimes and quarters, returned to the hot, ill-smelling telephone booth and proceeded to lay down a barrage of telephone calls to the B. Cohns of all towns of any importance contiguous to San Francisco Bay. And he was lucky. On the sixth call he located the particular B. Cohn in San Rafael, only to be informed by Mr. Cohn's cook that Mr. Cohn was dining at the home of a Mr. Simons in Mill Valley.

There were three Mr. Simons in Mill Valley, and Peck called them all before connecting with the right one. Yes, Mr. B. Cohn was there. Who wished to speak to him? Mr. Heck? Oh, Mr. Lake! A silence. Then—Mr. Cohn says he doesn't know any Mr. Lake and wants to know the nature of your business. He is dining and doesn't like to be disturbed unless the matter is of grave importance."

"Tell him Mr. Peck wishes to speak to him on a matter of very great importance," wailed the ex-private.

"Mr. Metz? Mr. Ben Metz?"

"No, no, no. Peck—p-e-c-k."

"D-e-c-k?"

"No, P."

"C?"

"P."

"Oh, yes, E. E-what?"

"C-K–"

"Oh, yes, Mr. Eckstein."

"Call Cohn to the phone or I'll go over there on the next boat and kill you, you damned idiot," shrieked Peck. "Tell him his store is on fire."

That message was evidently delivered for almost instantly Mr. B. Cohn was puffing and spluttering into the phone.

"Iss dot der fire marshal?" he managed to articulate.

"Listen, Mr. Cohn. Your store is not on fire, but I had to say so in order to get you to the telephone. I am Mr. Peck, a total stranger to you. You have a blue vase in your shop window on Geary Street in San Francisco. I want to buy it and I want to buy it before seven forty-five tonight. I want you to come across the bay and open the store and sell me that vase."

"Such a business! Vot you think I am? Crazy?"

"No, Mr. Cohn, I do not. I'm the only crazy man talking. I'm crazy for that vase and I've got to have it right away."

"You know vot dot vase costs?" Mr. B. Cohn's voice dripped syrup.

"No, and I don't give a hoot what it costs. I want what I want when I want it. Do I get it?"

"Ve-ell, lemme see. Vot time iss it?" A silence while B. Cohn evidently looked at his watch. "It iss now a quarter of seven, Mr. Eckstein, und der nexd drain from Mill Valley don't leaf until eight o'clock. Dot vill get me to San Francisco at eight-fifty—und I am dining mit friends und haf just finished my soup."

"To hell with your soup. I want that blue vase."

"Vell, I tell you, Mr. Eckstein, if you got to have it, call up my head salesman, Herman Joost, in der Chilton Apardments—Prospect three-two-four-nine, und tell him I said he should come down right avay qvick und sell you dot blue vase. Goodbye, Mr. Eckstein."

And B. Cohn hung up.

Instantly Peck called Prospect 3249 and asked for Herman Joost. Mr. Joost's mother answered. She was desolated because Herman was not at home, but vouchsafed the information that he was dining at the country club. Which country club? She did not know. So Peck procured from the hotel clerk a list of the country clubs in and around San Francisco and started calling them up. At eight o'clock he was still being informed that Mr. Juice was not a member, that Mr. Luce wasn't in, that Mr. Coos had been dead three months and that Mr. Boos had played but eight holes when he received a telegram calling him back to New York. At the other clubs Mr. Joust was unknown.

"Licked," murmured Bill Peck, "but never let it be said that I didn't go down fighting. I'm going to heave a brick through that show window, grab the vase and run with it."

He engaged a taxicab and instructed the driver to wait for him at the corner of Geary and Stockton Streets. Also, he borrowed from the chauffeur a ball peen hammer. When he reached the art shop of B. Cohn, however, a policeman was standing in the doorway, violating the general orders of a policeman on duty by surreptitiously smoking a cigar.

"He'll nab me if I crack that window," the desperate Peck decided, and continued on down the street, crossed to the other side and came back. It was now dark and over the art shop B. Cohn's name burned in small red, white and blue electric lights.

And lo, it was spelled B. Cohen!

Ex-private William E. Peck sat down on a fire hydrant and cursed with rage. His weak leg hurt him, too, and for some damnable reason, the stump of his left arm developed the feeling that his missing hand was itchy.

"The world is filled with idiots," he raved furiously. "I'm tired and I'm hungry. I skipped luncheon and I've been too busy to think of dinner."

He walked back to his taxicab and returned to the hotel where, hope springing eternal in his breast, he called Prospect 3249 again and discovered that the missing Herman Joost had returned to the bosom of his family. To him the frantic Peck delivered the message of B. Cohn, whereupon the cautious Herman Joost replied that he would confirm the authenticity of the message by telephoning to Mr. Cohn at Mr. Simon's home in Mill Valley. If Mr. B. Cohn or Cohen confirmed Mr. Kek's story he, the said Herman Joost, would be at the store sometime before nine o'clock, and if Mr. Kek cared to, he might await him there.

Mr. Kek said he would be delighted to wait for him there.

At nine-fifteen Herman Joost appeared on the scene. On his way down the street he had taken the precaution to pick up a policeman and bring him along with him. The lights were switched on in the store and Mr. Joost lovingly abstracted the blue vase from the window.

"What's the cursed thing worth?" Peck demanded.

"Two thousand dollars," Mr. Joost replied without so much as the quiver of an eyelash. "Cash," he added, apparently as an afterthought.

The exhausted Peck leaned against the sturdy guardian of the law and sighed. This was the final straw. He had about ten dollars in his possession.

"You refuse, absolutely, to accept my check?" he quavered.

"I don't know you, Mr. Peck," Herman Joost replied simply.

"Where's your telephone?"

Mr. Joost led Peck to the telephone and the latter called up Mr. Skinner.

"Mr. Skinner," he announced, "this is all that is mortal of Bill Peck speaking. I've got the store open and for two thousand dollars—cash—I can buy the blue vase Mr. Ricks has set his heart upon."

"Oh, Peck, dear fellow," Mr. Skinner purred sympathetically. "Have you been all this time on that errand?"

"I have. And I'm going to stick on the job until I deliver the goods. For God's sake let me have two thousand dollars and bring it down to me at B. Cohen's Art Shop on Geary Street near Grant Avenue. I'm too utterly exhausted to go up after it."

"My dear Mr. Peck, I haven't two thousand dollars in my house. That is too great a sum of money to keep on hand."

"Well, then, come downtown, open up the office safe and get the money for me."

"Time lock on the office safe, Peck. Impossible."

"Well then, come downtown and identify me at hotels and cafés and restaurants so I can cash my own check."

"Is your check good, Mr. Peck?"

The flood of invective which had been accumulating in Mr. Peck's system all the afternoon now broke its bounds. He screamed at Mr. Skinner a blasphemous invitation to betake himself to the lower regions.

"Tomorrow morning," he promised hoarsely, "I'll beat you to death with the stump of my left arm, you miserable, cold-blooded, lazy, shiftless slacker."

He called up Cappy Ricks' residence next, and asked for Captain Matt Peasley, who, he knew, made his home with his father-in-law. Matt Peasley came to the telephone and listened sympathetically to Peck's tale of woe.

"Peck, that's the worst outrage I ever heard of," he declared. "The idea of setting you such a task. You take my advice and forget the blue vase."

"I can't," Peck panted. "Mr. Ricks will feel mighty chagrined if I fail to get the vase to him. I wouldn't disappoint him for my right arm. He's been a dead game sport with me, Captain Peasley."

"But it's too late to get the vase to him, Peck. He left the city at eight o'clock and it is now almost half past nine."

"I know, but if I can secure legal possession of the vase I'll get it to him before he leaves the train at Santa Barbara at six o'clock tomorrow morning."

"How?"

"There's a flying school out at the Marina and one of the pilots there is a friend of mine. He'll fly to Santa Barbara with me and the vase."

"You're crazy."

"I know it. Please lend me two thousand dollars."

"What for?"

"To pay for the vase."

"Now I know you're crazy—or drunk. Why if Cappy Ricks ever forgot himself to the extent of paying two hundred dollars for a vase he'd bleed to death in an hour."

"Won't you let me have two thousand dollars, Captain Peasley?"

"I will not, Peck, old son. Go home and to bed and forget it."

"Please. You can cash your checks. You're known so much better than I, and it's Sunday night—"

"And it's a fine way to keep holy the Sabbath day," Matt Peasley retorted and hung up.

"Well," Herman Joost queried, "do we stay here all night?"

Bill Peck bowed his head. "Look here," he demanded suddenly, "do you know a good diamond when you see it?"

"I do," Herman Joost replied.

"Will you wait here until I go to my hotel and get one?"

"Sure."

Bill Peck limped painfully away. Forty minutes later he returned with a platinum ring set with diamonds and sapphires.

"What are they worth?" he demanded.

Herman Joost looked the ring over lovingly and appraised it conservatively at twenty-five hundred dollars.

"Take it as security for the payment of my check," Peck pleaded. "Give me a receipt for it and after my check has gone through clearing I'll come back and get the ring."

Fifteen minutes later, with the blue vase packed in excelsior and reposing in a stout cardboard box, Bill Peck entered a restaurant and ordered dinner. When he had dined he engaged a taxi and was driven to the flying field at the Marina. From the night watchman he ascertained the address of his pilot friend and at midnight, with his friend at the wheel, Bill Peck and his blue vase soared up into the moonlight and headed south.

An hour and a half later they landed in a stubble field in the Salinas Valley and, bidding his friend good-bye, Bill Peck trudged across to the railroad track and sat down. When the train bearing Cappy Ricks came roaring down the valley, Peck twisted a Sunday paper with which he had provided himself, into an improvised torch, which he lighted. Standing between the rails he swung the flaming paper frantically.

The train slid to a halt, a brakeman opened a vestibule door, and Bill Peck stepped wearily aboard.

"What do you mean by flagging this train?" the brakeman demanded angrily, as he signaled the engineer to proceed. "Got a ticket?"

"No, but I've got the money to pay my way. And I flagged this train because I wanted to change my method of travel. I'm looking for a man in stateroom A of car 7, and if you try to block me there'll be murder done."

"That's right. Take advantage of your half-portion arm and abuse me," the brakeman retorted bitterly. "Are you looking for that little old man with the Henry Clay collar and the white mutton-chop whiskers?"

"I certainly am."

"Well, he was looking for you just before we left San Francisco. He asked me if I had seen a one-armed man with a box under his good arm. I'll lead you to him."

A prolonged ringing at Cappy's stateroom door brought the old gentleman to the entrance in his nightshirt.

"Very sorry to have to disturb you, Mr. Ricks," said Bill Peck, "but the fact is there were so many Cohens and Cohns and Cohans, and it was such a job to dig up two thousand dollars, that I failed to connect with you at seven forty-five last night, as per orders. It was absolutely impossible for me to accomplish the task within the time limit set, but I was resolved that you should not be disappointed. Here is the vase. The shop wasn't within four blocks of where you thought it was, sir, but I'm sure I found the right vase. It ought to be. It cost enough and was hard enough to get, so it should be precious enough to form a gift for any friend of yours."

Cappy Ricks stared at Bill Peck as if the latter were a wraith.

"By the Twelve Ragged Apostles!" he murmured. "By the Holy Pink-toed Prophet! We changed the sign on you and we stacked the Cohens on you and we set a policeman to guard the shop to keep you from breaking the window, and we made you dig up two thousand dollars on Sunday night in a town where you are practically unknown, and while you missed the train at eight o'clock, you overtake it at two o'clock in the morning and deliver the blue vase. Come in and rest your poor old game leg, Bill. Brake-man, I'm much obliged to you."

Bill Peck entered and slumped wearily down on the settee. "So it was a plant?" he cracked, and his voice trembled with rage. "Well, sir, you're an old man and you've been good to me, so I do not begrudge you your little joke, but Mr. Ricks, I can't stand things like I used to. My leg hurts and my stump hurts and my heart hurts—"

He paused, choking, and the tears of impotent rage filled his eyes. "You shouldn't treat me that way, sir," he complained presently. "I've been trained not to question orders, even when they seem utterly foolish to me; I've been trained to obey them—on time, if possible, but if impossible, to obey them anyhow. I've been taught loyalty to my chief—and I'm sorry my chief found it necessary to make a buffoon of me. I haven't had a very good time the past three years and—and—you can—pa-pa-pass your skunk spruce and larch rustic and short odd length stock to some slacker like Skinner—and you'd better arrange to replace Skinner, because he's young enough to take a beating—and I'm going to give it to him—and it'll be a hospital job, sir—"

Cappy Ricks ruffled Bill Peck's aching head with a paternal hand.

"Bill, old boy, it was cruel—damnably cruel, but I had a big job for you and I had to find out a lot of things about you before I entrusted you with that job. So I arranged to give you the Degree of the Blue Vase, which is the supreme test of a go-getter. You thought you carried into this stateroom a two thousand dollar vase, but between ourselves, what you really carried in was a ten thousand dollar job as our Shanghai manager."

"Wha—what!"

"Every time I have to pick out a permanent holder of a job worth ten thousand dollars, or more, I give the candidate the Degree of the Blue Vase," Cappy explained. "I've had two men out of a field of fifteen deliver the vase, Bill."

Bill Peck had forgotten his rage, but the tears of his recent fury still glistened in his bold blue eyes. "Thank you, sir. I forgive you—and I'll make good in Shanghai."

"I know you will, Bill. Now, tell me, son, weren't you tempted to quit when you discovered the almost insuperable obstacles I'd placed in your way?"

"Yes, sir, I was. I wanted to commit suicide before I'd finished telephoning all the C-o-h-e-n-s in the world. And when I started on the C-o-h-n-s—well, it's this way, sir. I just couldn't quit because that would have been disloyal to a man I once knew."

"Who was he?" Cappy demanded, and there was awe in his voice.

"He was my brigadier, and he had a brigade motto: *It shall be done.* When the divisional commander called him up and told him to move forward with his brigade and occupy certain territory, our brigadier would say: 'Very well, sir. It shall be done.' If any officer in his brigade showed signs of flunking his job because it appeared impossible, the brigadier would just look at him once—and then that officer would remember the motto and go and do his job or die trying.

"In the army, sir, the *esprit de corps* doesn't bubble up from the bottom. It filters down from the top. An organization is what its commanding officer is—neither better nor worse. In my company, when the top sergeant handed out a week of kitchen police to a buck, that buck was out of luck if he couldn't muster a grin and say: 'All right, sergeant. It shall be done.'

"The brigadier sent for me once and ordered me to go out and get a certain German sniper. I'd been pretty lucky— some days I got enough for a mess—and he'd heard of me. He opened a map and said to me: 'Here's about where he holes up. Go get him, Private Peck.' Well, Mr. Ricks, I snapped into it and gave him a rifle salute, and said, 'Sir, it shall be done'—and I'll never forget the look that man gave me. He came down to the field hospital to see me after I'd walked into one of those Austrian 88's. I knew my left wing was a total loss and I suspected my left leg was about to leave me, and I was downhearted and wanted to die. He came and bucked me up. He said: 'Why, Private Peck, you aren't half dead. In civil life you're going to be worth half a dozen live ones—aren't you?' But I was pretty far gone and I told him I didn't believe it, so he gave me a hard look and said: 'Private Peck will do his utmost to recover and as a starter he will smile.' Of course, putting it in the form of an order, I had to give him the usual reply, so I grinned and said: 'Sir, it shall be done.' He was quite a man, sir, and his brigade had a soul—his soul—"

"I see, Bill. And his soul goes marching on, eh? Who was he, Bill?"

Bill Peck named his idol.

"By the Twelve Ragged Apostles!" There was awe in Cappy Ricks' voice, there was reverence in his faded old eyes. "Son," he continued gently, "twenty-five years ago your brigadier was a candidate for an important job in my employ—and I gave him the Degree of the Blue Vase. He couldn't get the vase legitimately, so he threw a cobble-stone through the window, grabbed the vase and ran a mile and a half before the police captured him. Cost me a lot of money to square the case and keep it quiet. But he was too good, Bill, and I couldn't stand in his way; I let him go forward to his destiny. But tell me, Bill. How did you get the two thousand dollars to pay for this vase?"

"Once," said ex-Private Peck thoughtfully, "the brigadier and I were first at a dug-out entrance. It was a headquarters dug-out and they wouldn't surrender, so I bombed them and then we went down. I found a finger with a ring on it—and the brigadier said if I didn't take the ring somebody else would. I left that ring as security for my check."

"But how could you have the courage to let me in for a two thousand dollar vase? Didn't you realize that the price was absurd and that I might repudiate the transaction?"

"Certainly not. You are responsible for the acts of your servant. You are a true blue sport and would never repudiate my action. You told me what to do, but you did not insult my intelligence by telling me how to do it. When my late brigadier sent me after the German sniper he didn't take into consideration the probability that the sniper might get me. He told me to get the sniper. It was my business to see to it that I accomplished my mission and carried my objective, which, of course, I could not have done if I had permitted the German to get me."

"I see, Bill. Well, give that blue vase to the porter in the morning. I paid fifteen cents for it in a five, ten and fifteen cent store. Meanwhile, hop into that upper berth and help yourself to a well-earned rest."

"But aren't you going to a wedding anniversary at Santa Barbara, Mr. Ricks?"

"I am not. Bill, I discovered a long time ago that it's a good idea for me to get out of town and play golf as often as I can. Besides which, prudence dictates that I remain away from the office for a week after the seeker of blue vases fails to deliver the goods and—by the way, Bill, what sort of a game do you play? Oh, forgive me, Bill. I forgot about your left arm."

"Say, look here, sir," Bill Peck retorted, "I'm big enough and ugly enough to play one-handed golf."

"But, have you ever tried it?"

"No, sir," Bill Peck replied seriously, "but—it shall be done!"

Conclusion

The Blueprint of the Doer

Make It Happen is more than a title—it's a call to action. It's a mindset, a personal code, and a challenge to rise above mediocrity.

Both *A Message to Garcia* and *The Go-Getter* remind us that success rarely depends on genius, connections, or luck. It depends on *you*—on your character, your willingness to act, your ability to persevere when the path is unclear, and your refusal to quit.

So what will you do with the message you've just received?

There are Garcias in the world who need your help. There are blue vases waiting to be delivered. Whether you're leading a team, starting a business, or building your life—don't wait. Don't ask for a map. Get up. Move forward. Go make it happen.

About Elbert Hubbard

Elbert Green Hubbard (1856–1915) was an American writer, publisher, artist, and philosopher. Raised in Hudson, Illinois, Hubbard is known best as the founder of the Roycroft artisan community in East Aurora, New York, an influential exponent of the Arts and Crafts movement.

Among Hubbard's many publications were the fourteen-volume work *Little Journeys to the Homes of the Great* and the short publication "A Message to Garcia." He and his second wife, Alice Moore Hubbard, died aboard the RMS Lusitania when it was torpedoed and sunk by German submarine SM U-20 off the coast of Ireland on May 7, 1915.

About
Peter B. Kyne

P eter Bernhard Kyne (1880–1957) was an American novelist from San Francisco, California who published sixteen novels between 1913 and 1936. More than 100 of his works were adapted into screenplays beginning in the silent film era, many of the earliest without consent or compensation. His first novel, *The Three Godfathers*, was published in 1913 and has been repeatedly adapted in film and television.

Kyne served in the Philippines with Company L, 14th U.S. Infantry from 1898 to 1899. During World War I, he served as a captain of Battery A of the California National Guard 144th Field Artillery Regiment.

At the age of 27, Kyne got into heavy debts running a retail furnishing goods business, which led him to attempt suicide. He fired a pistol into his chest, but was spared by a defective cartridge. He then settled with his creditors and his first book was published six years later.

The Go-Getter was his eighth novel, published in 1922, and adapted into a film in 1937.

THANK YOU FOR READING THIS BOOK!

If you found any of the information helpful, please take a few minutes and leave a review on the bookselling platform of your choice.

BONUS GIFT!

Don't forget to sign up to try our newsletter and grab your free personal development ebook here:

soundwisdom.com/classics